SW

IN THE PEDLAR'S FOOTSTEPS

'YE PEDLAR OF SWAFFHAM WHO DID BY A DREAM FIND A GREAT TREASURE'

So says the legend on the town sign in Swaffham Market Place. What is the story behind this?

Our tale begins around the middle of the 15th century when one John Chapman reputedly earned his living in the town as a pedlar.

One night John had a dream that if he should go to London Bridge he would hear good news. John did not take much notice of this, but he had the same dream several times and eventually decided to find out what it was all about. With a pack on his back and accompanied by his dog, John set off for London. It was a long and hazardous journey in those days, with danger not from traffic, but from footpads and highwaymen.

Eventually, John arrived safely on London Bridge. There he waited to hear his 'good news'. For days he walked the bridge waiting and listening, but hearing nothing that was of any use. Not, that is, until a shopkeeper became interested in this stranger who was walking up and down the bridge for no apparent reason. What was he doing? The shopkeeper went out and asked him. John told him about his dream and how he had decided to see what it was all about. The shopkeeper laughed. 'What a silly idea! If I took any notice of my dreams, I would never get any work done. Why, only last night I dreamt that if I went to a little place called Swaffham, somewhere in Norfolk, and dug under an apple tree, I would find lots of treasure. Do you think I am fool enough to believe that? Of course not! If I were you my friend, I would go home and not take any notice of your dreams.'

John, realising that this was the news he had been waiting for, did not say any more, but thanked the shopkeeper for his advice and set off back to Swaffham.

When he arrived home, he immediately dug under the apple tree in his garden. Sure enough, there was the treasure – a big brass pot full of gold coins. After John had removed these coins, he put the empty pot amongst his wares. A friend saw it and read the inscription on it, which John himself could not read. This inscription told of another much larger vessel beneath the first.

John set to work once more, digging beneath the apple tree and the message on the first pot was soon proved genuine, for there was the other one, much bigger as foretold, again full of treasure.

With his new-found wealth, John Chapman paid to have the north aisle of the parish church rebuilt as part of a reconstruction programme. He also paid part of the cost of rebuilding the tower, as well as making other generous gifts.

That is the story of the Pedlar of Swaffham, but what are the facts?

It is known that a John Chapman did live in the town and that he was a churchwarden in 1462 at the time of the rebuilding of the church. It is also recorded that he gave a lot of money towards rebuilding the north aisle and the tower of the church. We also believe we know where John's house was, and on that site today is the splendid Elizabethan house, with a Georgian facade, known as *'Oakleigh House'*. The town's pedlar sign is just across the road.

The story of the Pedlar of Swaffham was told in its present form at least as long ago as 1652, when Sir William Dugdale referred to it in a letter to Sir Roger Twysden. The legend has remained much the same ever since.

These are all facts, but the part of the story which we can neither prove nor disprove is the way in which our pedlar came by his wealth. The dream story could have been thought up to cover up wealth obtained by not totally honest means, such as gold smuggling. Alternatively, John could have found what might have been Roman or Saxon buried treasure under the apple tree when he was digging his garden. Even today people find treasure trove in all sorts of places.

Or he could have had a dream . . .

Swaffham's famous Pedlar sign with its creator, the late Harry Carter. The Pedlar sign was the first of over 100 he carved for towns and villages in the region. (Courtesy of Mrs M Carter)

A very famous story, the Pedlar of Swaffham has been featured in many books, on television a few times and on a record by Sir Bernard Miles. The Pedlar is commemorated in Swaffham in many ways. Postcards, bookmarks and other mementoes are available, and some shops incorporate the Pedlar in their name. The most obvious reference is the town sign, carved in wood by Harry Carter, who was well-known in the region for this craft. Swaffham's magnificent parish church has carved clergy stalls and pew ends representing the pedlar and until the last century had stained glass windows in his honour, but these were badly damaged in a gale and now only fragments remain.

THE BEGINNINGS OF THE TOWN

People may have lived in and around Swaffham long before it acquired the name we know it by today. New Stone Age (Neolithic) flint tools are often found in and around the fields and gardens of the town. In fact, one of the largest flint cores found in the region came from just outside the town. This is a stone from which flakes were taken to shape axes, arrowheads and tools.

The reasons Neolithic people were here may not be immediately apparent, for there was no running water for miles, although there was a substantial area of wetland to the north of the town and Neolithic artefacts have been found in this area too. No traces of buildings or pottery have been discovered so we cannot be sure if there was a settlement there, although the abundance of worked flints would suggest that there was. Even so, it would normally only have been for a short time, while the land around was cleared of trees and then farmed until the soil was exhausted. The farmers would then move on and the old site left to recover, when it would be used again.

These people, besides being the first to work the land, were also the first to keep domestic animals and it was these animals, grazing over the land recently abandoned after cultivation, that prevented regeneration of the woodlands and so helped to create the large tracts of heath around the town and elsewhere in Breckland.

To stay here for any length of time, there must have been certain advantages for the nomadic Neolithic farmer and these were that the site was high and dry and this height also gave a strategic advantage over enemies.

Artefacts from a very much earlier age are often found in the gravel excavations along the Nar valley. These Old Stone Age (Palaeolithic) tools are between three and four hundred thousand years old and were deposited by glacial action during one of the Ice Ages. These are not normally found in Swaffham, though there can be little doubt that the primitive men who used these flints roamed around here.

Evidence of Bronze Age occupation has often been found in and around the town and the burial mounds, or *'barrows'* just to the south, on what used to be Pickenham Heath, were the judicial courts of the Hundred of South Greenhoe. In Blomefield's *'History of Norfolk'*, it is stated that these barrows were used for this purpose until about 1725. These places were considered sacred, an oath made on a barrow being the equivalent of one made on a Bible today.

This particular Hundred stretches from Newton-by-Castleacre in the north to Didlington in the south, and from Narborough in the west to East Bradenham in the east. The Pickenham barrows are in a fairly central position in this area.

The Romans were here too, for coins and fragments of tiles and pottery have been found in and around the town. Unfortunately no remains of any size have been found as yet.

This cannot be said of the Swabians who came after. Three schools of thought debate the nature of their coming. One idea is that they were invaders, burning and plundering their way across the country, destroying evidence of Roman culture as they went. One alternative, which is far more likely, is that they integrated into local society, changing things much more gradually. The third possibility is that they were remnants of the once powerful Roman army, former colonial soldiers who had decided to stay after the collapse of the Roman Empire. These people from Germany possibly gave their name to the town, for Swaffham, 'homestead of the Swabians', is likely to have been the name given to an Anglo Saxon settlement here, dating back to the 5th century. This, in turn, was perhaps the name given to describe a previous Swabian community, although no evidence of this has come to light. If Swaffham had an earlier name, it has since been lost.

A major piece of evidence for Saxon habitation is at the *'Paddocks'* where a 6th century Pagan-Saxon burial ground was found in 1970. Although the tall, fair Saxons were a different race from the shorter, dark, Swabians, the people in the cemetery may well have included the direct descendants of the original Swabian settlers who had integrated into the local society and became virtually indistinguishable, both culturally and physically. The site, which is off Haspalls Road, has only been partially excavated and what remains beneath the soil can only be guessed at. Earlier burials may still be covered over by roads and houses.

Many fine and important artefacts buried with the deceased in the 6th century AD were discovered in 1970 during the construction of a housing estate. Most of these are now in Norwich Castle Museum, where some are on view. A few others are on display in Swaffham Mus..

After conversion to Christianity, it is possible that the Saxons built the first stone church in the town. There are other Saxon stone churches still standing in the area and it would seem likely that Swaffham had such a church.

The Normans had the task of recording as much as they could in the Domesday Book and Swaffham was credited in 1086 as having, amongst other things, twelve pigs, four cows, two rounceys (working horses), one and a half mills (the half probably meant that it was shared with another village) and a fishpond. The mills are interesting as windmills had not been introduced then, although watermills had arrived with the Romans. However, if they were watermills that would mean the town would have had mills sited at some distance outside the parish, possibly at Narborough, or along the River Nar. It is more likely that the mills referred to were hand, or even animal driven, one being in the town and the half shared with a nearby hamlet, such as St Guthlac Stow.

It was the Domesday Book that first recorded the fact that there were two manors in Swaffham. One of these was probably the Manor of Swaffham, held by Harold, Earl of Kent, from 1042 to 1066 when, as King Harold, he was killed. The other manor could have been the Manor of Aspalls (sic), although the first mention of that was not until 1239. The Manor of Whitsands possibly derived its name from the owner in 1273, the first time this particular manor is mentioned.

The Normans and their descendants held the actual Manor of Swaffham for 250 years. The title still exists today, although the manorial rights are virtually non-existent. The combined manors of Haspalls and Whitsands are now part of the Town Estate, having been given to the town by Simon Blake in his will of 1487. They provide an income for the church, pensions for the townspeople and grants.

SWAFFHAM CHURCH

The building of the present church commenced in 1454 on the site of a previous, possibly Saxon, church which had finally collapsed. There is no remaining visible evidence of the architecture of the old building; the flints from the old walls would probably have been re-used in new walls. Other materials, referred to as *'thack'* in contemporary documents, were sold off.

The superb Early English church we see today is one of the finest in the county, with its truly magnificent double hammerbeam roof and spacious interior. Entering the church the east window immediately strikes the eye. Large and colourful, it was the gift of the Day family, of the Norwich and

A print of the church by Samuel John Carter. This shows the old church clock, but not the old vicarage, which stood between the road and the church. It must therefore have been drawn between 1847 when the old vicarage was demolished and 1856 when the clock was replaced.

Swaffham Bank, in the last century. It has been said that this window is rather out of character with the rest of the church, but with the sun shining through it in the early morning it is an attractive example of Victorian stained glass.

On the left, as we walk down the aisle, is a commemorative plaque to W J Donthorn, the Swaffham born architect who designed the Leicester Memorial column at Holkham Hall. Donthorn was one of the founder members of the Royal Institute of British Architects.

On the right is Corpus Christi chapel with a memorial window and tablet to the fallen of the First World War. This window was designed by Rev Keeling-Scott and, it is said, Sir Arthur Knyvet Wilson Bt VC, who also helped in the design of the tablet. A memorial plaque to Sir Arthur is in the chapel, with a copy of his citation. He was born in Swaffham and is buried in the churchyard.

Just past Corpus Christi chapel is the Lady Chapel and in the corner is a statue of Catherine Steward of Swaffham, who was Oliver Cromwell's maternal grandmother.

In the floor before the altar is a memorial slab to

family, an arms-bearing family with connections in the town. The 11 volume epic 'History of Norfolk' by Francis Blomefield was published in the early 19th century and is still considered a very valuable reference book for local historians.

Beside the altar lies the tomb of John Botewright DD, the rector responsible for the rebuilding of the church. He was chaplain to Henry VI and Master of Corpus Christi College, Cambridge. This explains the pelicans on the pew ends; they are the symbol of that college.

Although he was chaplain to the King and had many other interests, Rev Botewright campaigned on behalf of the townspeople of Swaffham against greedy and grasping landlords, including the Duchy of Lancaster. Dr Botewright's affection for Swaffham is also reflected in the gift of land he made to the town. Known as *'The Campingland'*, this was given in April 1463 for sport, military drill and other *'honest games'*. This may be because, according to Blomefield, the rector 'was born in this town of Swaffham'. The rector was also responsible for writing the *'Black Book of Swaffham'*, the second oldest church terrier in existence. This extremely interesting record dates from 1454 and is today kept safely locked away in a bank vault.

Close to Dr Botewright's tomb is a memorial plaque to the Old Boys of Hamond's School who lost their lives in the last war.

Another memorial is to Henry Lee Warner, governor of Hamond's School. He attended Rugby School as a pupil from 1854, when the classic story *'Tom Brown's Schooldays'* was written, then went to St John's College, Cambridge, where he was a distinguished classical scholar. Amongst his achievements was the winning of the Bachelor Members' Prize in 1865 and becoming a Fellow of his college the same year. Henry Lee Warner MA went back to Rugby as an assistant master under Dr Temple in 1864 and taught there until 1887.

The old vicarage by Samuel John Carter. Drawn in 1846, when Samuel was 11 years old.

Outside the church, on the east side of the churchyard lie some of the town's most famous sons. Sir Arthur Knyvet Wilson Bt VC, Samuel John Carter and his son, William Carter RA.

The small cottage in the churchyard is possibly one of the oldest buildings in the town. The Rev Gilbert Bouchery wrote in 1730 that it was first of all a Guild House, until the suppression of the guilds in 1534 during the reformation by Henry VIII. The crossed keys in the brickwork of the older of the two chimneys, suggests this might have been the house of the Guild of St Peter, although the Rev Bouchery thought that it was probably a meeting house for more than one guild.

Blomefield tells us there were seven guilds in Swaffham, each dedicated to a patron saint, and these served a number of purposes. They were voluntary associations, where members paid contributions, worshipped together, often in their particular guild chapel in the church, feasted together, aided each other in sickness and poverty and contributed to good causes. The guilds grew in importance and influence. They could purchase land, build chapels, erect altars and maintain chaplains. The Guild of the Holy Trinity was the wealthiest of the Swaffham guilds and had a piscina, or holy water basin, near the altar, which is still there today. There are two other piscinas in the church, one near the organ and one in the Lady Chapel, but the origins of these are unknown.

The Guild of Ascension was also wealthy, owning much land, but the Guild of St Peter, with which the Church Cottage is said to be connected, was relatively poor and yet was apparently wealthy enough to own a cottage. After the suppression of these guilds this cottage became a schoolhouse and remained so until the last century. From then until 1988 it served as the verger's cottage.

At the front of the church again, the large clock can be seen on the tower. Donated by Colonel Mason of Necton Hall in 1856, it is still wound by hand; one of the winders today is the third successive generation of his family to hold this position.

THE MARKET PLACE

Leaving the church and walking back down Church Walk into town, the Corn Exchange comes immediately into view across the road. Now government offices, it was built to accommodate the corn dealing that had previously been conducted in the White Hart Inn. It was built on behalf of the Swaffham Corn Exchange and Public Rooms Company in 1858 by a local builder, Mathias Goggs. Mr Goggs built a very substantial red and white brick building in the Italian style for £1,460. During its long and varied life it has served as a concert hall, meeting room, library, men's club, Salvation Army citadel and the armoury for the Norfolk Regiment 3rd Volunteer Battalion. Joseph Arch, the founder of the National Union of Agricultural Labourers, spoke here during the last century.

On this site originally was the Mansion House. Not, as one might imagine, a grand house owned by some local dignitary, but a better sort of public house or hotel.

Close to the Mansion House was the Cross or Market House, which was quite a substantial building. It was erected in 1575 by Robert Stapleton, vicar of Swaffham. Open on three sides, the Market House had a courthouse on the first floor and two shops on the ground floor. It was demolished in 1783 and the war memorial now stands on that site.

Across the road, where now stands a rather ordinary looking 1950s flat-roofed building, was *'The Crown'*, once the premier coaching inn of the town, Lady Hamilton entertained here when in Swaffham with the Nelsons. *'The Crown'* was also the meeting place of many local clubs and societies, such as the coursing club, but the *'Swaffham Rat Society'*, a sort of poor man's sporting club, met at the George Hotel.

One of the founder members of the Rat Society rejoiced in the name of *'Squire Fatsides'*, and the requirements for membership were just a terrier-type dog or a ferret. The club members wore a blue necktie and the club fare was bread, cheese and beer. Known to exist in 1823, the club had died out long before the 1890s, but in its heyday the 60 members killed thousands of rats every year, much to the delight of the local farmers.

The Crown Inn premises. The part of the hotel occupied in the photograph by 'Buntings' is the only part still standing. It is now a shoe shop. The main part of the hotel to the left of the picture was pulled down in the 1950s because it had started to collapse into its own very large cellars. Buntings was a successful business and later occupied the shop on the right. At one time the Bunting family employed nearly one hundred people and ran a successful mail order company from here.

THE MARKET CROSS AND 18TH CENTURY FAME

The present Market Cross was built in 1783 for George, Earl of Orford, grandson of Sir Robert Walpole. It is one of the town's most famous landmarks and has a statue of Ceres, the goddess of corn and agriculture, mounted on the top. The statue cost £200, half the cost of the whole building. In 1786 the Earl was responsible for founding the Swaffham Coursing Club. This, the first such club in the country, is still in existence today. The earliest known programme, which dates from 1789, is in the Norfolk Record Office. It may be that this club was the first to hold organised greyhound racing in this country. On the other side of the road, the *'Blue Belle'* public house was probably renamed *'The Greyhound'* in honour of the Earl and the name survives today.

The Market Cross is also known as the *'Butter Cross'*. Trading in butter went on under the roof of this building and W H Kemble wrote in 1833 that during the 18th century much local butter went to London under the general name of *'Cambridge Butter'*. 90,000 firkins (quarter barrel) were reported as being despatched annually. Today the Market Cross is a scheduled ancient monument.

The Assembly Rooms, which face the Market Cross, have been extensively renovated since the war, but they are still very similar to how they were in the 18th century when Swaffham was a great social centre in West Norfolk. Beautiful chandeliers once hung from the ceiling and the walls were covered with paintings. Now, sadly, only two 19th century works remain; a group of horses near water by Samuel John Carter, and a soldier, with the background possibly by Carter.

A jockey at the finishing post on Swaffham racecourse. The town can be seen in the distance (Courtesy of Grady's Country House Hotel)

The social importance of 18th century Swaffham can be demonstrated by the fact that in 1797 a cricket match was played here between 33 men of Norfolk and an England Eleven (England won!). The cricket pitch was in a clearing of 17 acres in the middle of the three mile long racecourse which twice crossed over the road to Cockley Cley. This racecourse was said to rival Newmarket for its light soil and panoramic views and was in existence from as far back as 1628 at least, making it one of the oldest in the country. The Prince of Wales (later George IV) raced here, and in 1789 won a gold cup donated by the Earl of Orford. Another occasional rider was Thomas Coke of Holkham Hall. Racing finished in Swaffham in about 1825.

The social *'season'*, which included the horseracing, also had other sporting diversions such as coursing on Swaffham Heath, at Marham and at Westacre, and cockfighting. The latter would be staged at the cockpit in Ash Close. Hundreds of pounds were won and lost here in what is now a quiet little side road off the Market Place.

In the evenings glittering balls were held at the Assembly Rooms. Many of the local nobility and gentry attended, including Lady Townshend of Raynham Hall, a very well known beauty of her day.

How highly the Assembly Rooms functions were regarded at the time is reflected in a local story told about two young ladies. They lived in the old Vicarage at Sporle, with their brother, Edmund Nelson. The ladies wished to go to a ball at the Assembly Rooms, but their brother forbade it. They were determined to go to this important event, and so decided to make their ballgowns in secret in their bedroom. In order that they should not be discovered, they blocked up the windows and the door of their bedroom. Unfortunately, they left no opening for ventilation and were found dead the next morning, presumably killed by fumes from the fire. They are buried together in Sporle churchyard.

At one time the Rev Edmund Nelson lived in Swaffham, on the left of what is now the Town Hall. Five of Edmund's children were christened in Swaffham church, including one Horatio. Unfortunately, little Horatio died very soon afterwards, but after Edmund was appointed vicar of Burnham Thorpe, he became father of another son, again christened Horatio, who went on to become one of our greatest sailors and a national hero.

Horatio maintained the family connection with Swaffham. His wife Fanny had set up home there whilst Horatio, then a captain, was away at sea. She had become bored with living at Burnham and decided that Swaffham was a much more interesting place to be.

On 2nd August 1806, Lord and Lady Nelson were staying in the town with their daughter and friends, including Lady Hamilton, and the *'Noble lord & his* party bespoke the play of She Stoops To Conquer'. It was reported that on this occasion the theatre was *'very generally filled'*. This lord was, however, the admiral's brother who had inherited the title after Horatio's death.

From 1824 the theatre was, naturally enough, down Theatre Street, known then as Back Lane. The theatre the Nelson's would have visited was the *'old'* one in Lynn Street, previously a barn, of which no trace remains. The Fisher family ran the theatre, one of many they owned in the county. In 1844, after the death of David Fisher, and during the general depression which followed the end of the Napoleonic Wars, it was sold. The site of the 'new' theatre is now occupied by the Swaffham Cue Club.

The Fisher Theatre, Back Lane. Taken when the building was used as the first Catholic church in Swaffham since the Reformation.

THE PLOWRIGHTS OF SWAFFHAM

Opposite the Assembly Rooms is a shopping precinct known as Plowright Place. Once the whole of this area was the site of the Plowright family's agricultural engineering business. Here was an iron foundry, a wheelwright, carpenters and all trades connected with the manufacture of horse ploughs, harrows and other farm equipment.

An old Swaffham family which can be traced back to 1457, the Plowrights kept business records dating from 1775 until the family sold the firm in 1939. It is likely that the family carried on its business there some time before the date of the oldest records, as a datestone at the back of the premises tells us JP (John Plowright?) owned the premises in 1746. The firm of Plowright still exists in the town under different ownership and the name is also used by the parent company for other agriculture-related businesses

To the right of Plowright Place and standing back from the road slightly is Fitzroy House, one of the best preserved Georgian houses in the town. Now the home of a number of small businesses, it was the offices of the Swaffham Rural District Council until 1974. Before that it belonged to the Plowright family and was visited a number of times by Queen Mary, a friend of Walter Cole Plowright. Mr Plowright was a local historian and antiquarian of some note who ran an antiques shop from here and Queen Mary, a collector of antiques, was interested in his collection.

If we carry on to the right of Fitzroy House, just past the modern bank are the former premises of the Norwich and Swaffham Bank, now the Swaffham Sixth Form Centre. High up on the wall can be seen the 1736 datestone removed from the old Hamond's Free School building on the Campingland. Although the Hamond name is now used for the Brandon Road High School, the datestone reminds us of the link with that name and all it has stood for here since 1901.

Next to the centre, on the corner, we come to the splendid Oakleigh House, an Elizabethan property with a Georgian front. This is the house referred to earlier as being on the probable site of the home of the Pedlar of Swaffham. Might there be yet another pot of gold in that garden?

Round this corner we cannot fail to notice a rather large rock, known as the Settlement Stone, standing all by itself on the pavement. The local stone, which so many of the older buildings incorporate in their walls, is flint, but this rock is a hard sandstone originating from Scandinavia. It probably found its way to this area as a stray rock carried along by glacial action and was then deposited as the ice receded at the end of one of the Ice Ages. It is likely that this specimen was found and brought here by the pagan Saxons. This rock, and others like it in other towns and villages, would have been regarded with some religious reverence by ancient peoples and would probably have been used as a central meeting place for the town. The manorial courts were held around the Stone, because an oath taken on it was as binding as an oath taken on the Bronze Age barrows on which the Hundred court was held.

Across the road from our Settlement Stone are the former buildings of the Swaffham Post Office. Built in 1894, the Post Office was here until 1968 when it moved across the road to the present building. In the early days of the penny post the town's first Stamp Office was in the small building next to the bus shelter.

Returning to the Market Place we must consider the Market itself. Indeed, on a Saturday it cannot be missed, with stalls on every possible empty space and a waiting list of traders to fill any vacant site, so popular is Swaffham's Saturday Market. Featured on television several times this, the biggest Saturday market in the region, has a long recorded history dating back to King

John. Probably long before that people sold their wares from improvised stalls on the green in the centre of town.

It may seem strange, but Swaffham Market might well have started on Sundays in the Church. This was the custom prior to the Norman Conquest and this enabled the inhabitants to carry out the duties of religion and trade together. Those attending the market had to swear that they would neither lie, steal or cheat; a precaution that was no doubt extremely necessary. A market in the church would have interfered with the religious service on a Sunday, so consequently would have been ousted into the churchyard and the day changed to Saturday. Eventually the market would have moved away from the church precincts and onto its present site.

The privilege of holding a market was granted during the reign of King John in about 1214, and confirmed by King Henry III in 1253, again during the reign of Edward I in 1286, and once more in 1308. This privilege meant that the market had some legal protection against other markets being set up in nearby villages.

A busy Swaffham fair day, in the 1850s. An important feature of this interesting photograph is the stall with the words 'YOUNG MACE' across the top. This was a boxing booth and Jem Mace (1831-1890) was World Boxing Champion in 1870. Known as the 'Swaffham Gipsy', Mace was the father of modern scientific boxing. He taught Lord Lonsdale the 'noble art' and also taught the Americans and the Australians how to box.

A later fair day, probably nearer the end of the century. (right)

The bottom of the schedule has the names of both the Lord of the Manor and of the Clerk to the old Urban District Council as joint administrators of the Market. (below)

Swaffham Market and Fairs.

Schedule of Market and Fair Stallages.

The Statutory Fairs are Second Wednesday in May, Third Wednesday in July, and First Wednesday in November.

		Market and Statutory Fairs Tolls		
		£	s.	d.
Cheap Jacks	per day		1	0
Cattle	per head			1
Circus	per day	1	5	0
Cocoanut Shies (not exceeding 15ft. × 16 ft.)	per day		2	6
Horses and Donkeys	per head			1
Inhabited Vans	per statutory fair day			1
„ „	other days			6
Herbalists and Medicine Vendors	per day		1	0
Roundabouts (other than steam)	one day		5	0
„ „ „	for every further day		2	6
„ (steam)	one day	1	0	0
„ „	for every further day		10	0
Stalls and Standings	frontage, per foot			1
Steam Engines and Threshing Tackle	per day		2	0
Steam Engines, Vans, Trucks and Timber Drugs (empty)	each, per day		1	0
Shooting Galleries (tunnels)	per day		1	6
„ „ (others)	per day		3	6
Sheep Pens	per hurdle			7
SHOWS:—				
Cinematographs	per day		10	0
Wild Beasts	per day	1	0	0
Other Shows	per day		5	0
Swinging Boats	per boat			6
"Try your Strength"	per day		1	0
Timber Drugs (loaded)	per day		2	0
Wood for Sale	per ton		1	0

NOTE.—For longer periods than two consecutive days or for tolls in respect of matters not scheduled above, special terms can be arranged with the Surveyor to the Council—MR. W. A. NORRIS, who is also the Collector of the Tolls.

By Order of the Urban District Council of Swaffham, and of the Lord of the Manor of Swaffham, and of the Honor of Richmond Fee.

(Signed) ALFRED JOHN WINTER,
Clerk to the Council.

(Signed) THOMAS A. H. HAMOND,
Lord of the Manor and Honor.

SWAFFHAM.

The Verdict of the Court Leet, holden this *Ninth* day of *June 1864*

FIRST.—We Amerce all Persons that lay Muck, or Straw to make Muck, in the Streets or Highways, or stop the common Drains, *Five Shillings* each offence, to the Lord of the Manor; and the Muck to be taken away by whoever thinks proper.

SECONDLY.—We Amerce all Persons that sell Flags out of Town, or dig Sand in the common Roads, or sell Stones, Gravel, Clay, or Sand, out of Town, *Five Shillings* per Load, each offence, to the Lord of the Manor.

THIRDLY.—We Amerce all Persons that cut or stub any Furze, or Ling, on the common, to sell out of Town, or burn Bricks with, *Five Shillings* per Load, each offence, half to the Lord of the Manor, and half to the Party or Parties giving information of the same, upon Conviction; and every Person setting fire to any Furze or Ling on the common Heath, *Five Pounds* each offence, to the Lord of the Manor.

FOURTHLY.—We Amerce all Persons that have Shepherds under them, that keep their Sheep staff-hold in the Lanes, *One Guinea* each offence, to the Lord of the Manor.

FIFTHLY.—We Amerce all Persons keeping neat Beasts, Horse, Mare, Colt, Filly or Ass, in the Highways or Lanes, except by Lines in hand, or Ropes staked at each end, and not across the High-ways, *Five Shillings* each offence, to the Lord of the Manor.

SIXTHLY.—We Amerce all Persons that Hawk with such Goods, as ought to stand in the Market, and all Huxters that Buy and Sell the same Goods again the same day, before Four o'clock in the Afternoon, *Five Shillings* each offence, to the Lord of the Manor.

SEVENTHLY.—We present all Persons washing Sheep within the Ponds in the Town; and all Drains into the said Ponds, or Drains from Muck-heaps or Privy-houses into the Streets, and all Waggons, Carts, Ploughs, &c., left standing in the Market-Place, Streets or Lanes, &c., *Ten Shillings* each offence, to the Lord of the Manor.

EIGHTLY.—We Amerce all Persons that stub up by the Roots, any Furze or Whins on the common Heath, otherwise than cutting them with a Hook or such like Instrument, above the ground, to forfeit *Five Shillings* for the quantity of twenty Fagots so stubbed, or cut up by the Roots, and a proportionate Penalty for every quantity above or under the said quantity of twenty Fagots, to the Lord of the Manor.

NINTHLY.—We Appoint *John Mash* Ale Taster, and *Wm Nusson and James Tooler* Clerks of the Market.

TENTHLY.—We Appoint *Thomas Jolls, John Ward, David Macrachne, George Ward, John Melton, John Bowers, Samuel Maxwell and George Greenwood*

In Pindars, and they shall have *Two Pence* per Head for ringing Swine, above 8 pounds weight, *Six-pence* per Head for Pounding them, and neat Beasts, Horses, Mares, Colts, Fillies, or Asses, as far as three in number, and *One Penny* per Head for all above that number, (though not all brought to Pound,) being found in the same Grounds, Highways or Lanes, except kept by the Rules in the fifth Article; and all Sheep found trespassing, *Six-Pence* per Score for Pounding them, as far as six Score, and *One Penny* per Score, for all above that number, though not all brought to Pound, and all Stock belonging to Non-residents, to be charged double Poundage.

ELEVENTHLY.—We Nominate and Appoint *Wm Grove* and Herdsmen, and they shall have *Six Pence* per Head per week, for keeping all sorts of Cattle, except young dry Stock and for these *Three-Pence* per Head.

The Herdsmen to go out with the Stock, from Lady to Michaelmas, at Seven o'clock in the Morning, and return at Six o'clock in the Evening; and from Michaelmas to Lady at Eight o'clock in the Morning, and return at Four o'clock in the Afternoon.

TWELFTHLY.—We present all Persons keeping Agist Cattle, taken from any other Parish, to be kept upon the common Pasture of this Parish, *Five Shillings* per Head for the first offence, for all Cattle so taken to Agist,—and *Ten Shillings* per Head, for the second and every other offence, to the Lord of the Manor.

We Amerce all Persons not belonging to the Parish, cutting Flags, Ling or Furze, *Ten Shillings* for each offence, to be paid to the Party giving information.

We present that there ought to be an open Road leading from Pickenham Lane, through Lodge-Path-Breck, siding South, commonly called Lodge-Path.

And we present all Persons digging Sand, Stones, Gravel, Clay or Earth, within Thirty feet of any Road *Ten Shillings* each offence, to the Lord of the Manor.

We Present Horrace Hudson of Swaffham for digging Sand within Thirty feet of the Road contrary to the Twelfth article

We Present Mr Benjamin Shanton for turning his neat Stock on the Common having no right to do so being contrary to the Fifth article

Poster – Penalties imposed in 1864 by the Court Leet, an elected body, the predecessor of the magistrates court. To amerce is to punish by a fine.

By 1620 Swaffham Market consisted of 133 stalls and 14 shops, though the number had fallen to 78 stalls by 1716. In 1833 W H Kemble wrote that *'At present a very small number of stalls and shambles (butchers' shops) constitute the decayed remains of its former consequence'*. The name 'Shambles' is still retained for the area behind the Assembly Rooms. Even as recently as this century, small shops still existed in this area. In 1888 one was recorded as being the premises of an *'emigration agent'* – a small but significant indication of how hard times were for many people then.

Livestock then, as now, was sold on Swaffham Market, mainly during the various fairs held throughout the year. Sheep, cattle and horses were the main animals on sale. These fairs were great social occasions and a cause of much absenteeism amongst the local schoolchildren during the last century, until eventually school holidays were granted on those days. The fairs died out in the early part of this century, but as recently as 1903 2,000 sheep were sold at the July fair. This compares with over 7,000 lambs in 1885. The origins of some of the fairs go back into antiquity and were related to special celebrations held in honour of the saints associated with the local church and on the anniversary of the consecration of that church. The locals spent the morning in church and the rest of the day eating and drinking and indulging in sports and rural pastimes.

Until relatively recently the rights to hold the market and fairs were held solely by the Lord of the Manor of Swaffham, but now the Town Council administers the whole market. It provides a substantial part of the town's income and is supervised by the Market Superintendent. A couple of hundred years ago it was considered necessary to annually appoint not only Clerks to the Market, but also Leather searchers, Leather sealers, Registers, Aletasters (a much sought-after position we can be sure!), Constables, Neatherds (cow-keepers) and Pinders. The Pinder was the person who would round up the stray animals and impound them. The owner would then have to pay to redeem the animal. The Pound still exists and can be seen down Mangate Street.

OTHER FESTIVITIES

Our forefathers certainly knew how to enjoy themselves on royal occasions as well as on religious festivals. For the coronation of William IV a whole ox was roasted, followed by plum pudding. The list shows the supplies laid on to celebrate the wedding of the Prince of Wales, later King Edward VII. As we can see by the day's schedule, the celebrations for the wedding of the Prince of Wales were held on the Market Place. The proceedings for the coronation of Queen Victoria in 1838 and her jubilee celebrations in 1887 were similar and a 19th century writer tells us that other celebrations held on the Hill were

SWAFFHAM DEMONSTRATION,

ON THE MARRIAGE OF

HIS R. H. THE PRINCE OF WALES.

MARCH 10TH, 1863.

DISBURSEMENTS.

	£.	s.	d.
150 Stone of MEAT, at 8s. 2d.	61	5	0
11 Barrels of BEER, at 36s.	20	12	0
Tables, Booth, Platform, &c. Messrs. Goggs £8 19s. Oakes £3 10s. Gainsborough £3.	15	9	0
FIREWORKS	12	0	0
Printing, Stationery, &c., Gooch £3 9s. 4d. Gould 18s 6d.	4	7	10

PUDDINGS.

	£.	s.	d.
37 Stone of Flour, at 2s.	3	14	0
5 ,, of Sugar, at 4s. 8d.	1	3	4
1 ,, of Salt, at 5d.	0	0	5
36 ,, of Raisins, at 5s. 6d.	9	18	0
2 lbs. of mixed Spice, at 3s.	0	6	0
12 Stone of Suet, at 8s. 2d.	4	18	0
172½ Yards of Calico, at 4½d	3	4	9

£23 4 6

POTATOES.

6 Sacks at 6s 6d.	1	19	0

BREAD.

36 Stone, at 2s.	3	12	0

BAKING.

162 Dishes, at 2d.	1	7	0

	£.	s.	d.
FLAGS	2	7	0
Rustic Sports	3	4	6
Ringers	1	0	0
Labor for Posts and Rails	0	11	8
Bonfire	0	9	6
Band	2	10	0
Sundries	1	12	6
Servants at Union	0	10	0

19 3 2

£156 1 6

Surely a day to remember!

SWAFFHAM FESTIVAL,

IN CELEBRATION OF THE MARRIAGE OF

H. R. H. THE PRINCE OF WALES.

TUESDAY, the 10th day of MARCH, 1863.

ORDER OF PROCEEDINGS.

First.—The day will be ushered in by the Ringing of Bells.

Second.—The Chairman, Stewards, Presidents of the Tables, the Rifle Corps, and it is hoped the Inhabitants generally, will assemble on the Hill at a quarter to ELEVEN o'clock, and proceed to CHURCH, where Divine Service appropriate to the day will be performed.

Third.—The Rifle Corps will parade and fire a Feu de Joie upon the Market Hill.

Fourth.—The Company to sit down at the several Tables agreeably to their respective Tickets, at Half-past TWELVE o'clock. Dinner to be on the Table at ONE precisely. On the sound of the Bugle, Grace will be said by the Vicar, every one to stand up uncovered, and silence to be kept.

Fifth.—The Stewards to be in their places, and Presidents and their Assistants, to be at their Tables at Half-past TWELVE o'clock; the Committee and Presidents to wear White Wedding Favors of Coventry Ribbon on their coats, the Assistants to wear a White Ribbon at their button holes, with a card of the number of the Table to which they belong.

Sixth.—Each President to furnish his respective Table with carving knife and fork, three dishes, saucers with salt, two saucers with mustard, two large spoons, two beer jugs, and provide two assistants.

Seventh.—Each person is requested to bring a knife, fork, plate, and a half-pint mug.—No baskets will be allowed.

Eighth.—The Stewards will superintend the distribution of Beer.

Ninth.—After dinner the following Toasts will be given on the sound of the Bugle, by the Chairman, and repeated by each President at his Table, when strict silence must be observed, in order that every one may distinctly hear them.

TOASTS.	MUSIC.
The QUEEN	God Save the QUEEN
The Prince and Princess of Wales	Haste to the Wedding
Prince Alfred and the rest of the Royal Family	Rule Britannia
The Army, Navy and the Volunteers	The British Grenadier
Prosperity to Swaffham	There's a Good Time Coming

Tables and Seats will then be removed, and at THREE o'clock RURAL SPORTS begin.

Tenth----At Dark a Display of FIREWORKS.

AFTER WHICH

A GRAND BON-FIRE.

☞ As a full quantity of Fuel will be provided, it is expected that none will think of adding to it, much less that any attempt at depredation will be made. Constables will be appointed to keep order:—at Half past TEN o'clock the fire will be extinguished and the Festival concluded.

The BALL at the Assembly Rooms to commence at 9. 30.

GOOCH, PRINTER, SWAFFHAM.

Celebrating Queen Victoria's Golden Jubilee in 1887

for the suppression of the rebellion in Scotland (a whole roast bullock), the end of the Napoleonic wars (roast beef and plum pudding, then rustic sports such as donkey racing, pig hunting etc., followed by a large bonfire and a grand display of fireworks) and for the coronation of William IV. In fact, it seems as if it did not need much encouragement at all for a really good knees-up on the Market Place!

The beer for these occasions might well have been provided by Morse's Brewery, (real Real Ale!) which stood just down Cley Road. The brewery has long since gone, but the brewer's house is now the Town Hall.

LAW AND ORDER

The stallholders who broke the market regulations may well have appeared in the courtroom of the Market House referred to earlier. After 1839, the Shirehall in White Cross Road (first on the left along London Street) was the venue for the local courts. Now containing flats, the Shirehall was built backing on to the Bridewell, or prison. From these courts many were deported for relatively minor offences and many upright citizens of the New World have traced their ancestry back to a harsh sentence handed out in the Shirehall.

When being brought before the court, the prisoners emerged from a hole in the floor of the courtroom and the public in the gallery must have thought that they were being brought up from the dungeons. In reality the prisoners had come along a short underground passage from cells at ground level. It would have been easy to provide a door through which prisoners could come, but the underground passage was more dramatic for the onlookers.

THE BRIDEWELL OR HOUSE OF CORRECTION

The prison, which faced London Street near the junction with White Cross Road, existed from 1599 until 1880 when, much to the relief of the local people, it was demolished. It had been rebuilt and enlarged a number of times. During the Napoleonic Wars a number of French prisoners of war were held here and they carved their names in the cell walls.

During the early part of the 19th century there was considerable unrest in the country and county and a contemporary report by a Mr Plowright exists in the Norfolk Records Office, telling of a plot which was discovered, to free the poachers in Swaffham jail. On May 16th 1816, the rioters were reported to have assembled at Downham and were ready to march to Swaffham. The order was issued to double-iron all prisoners, and a great many special constables were appointed, some standing guard during the night. The next day, the Swaffham troop of the Norfolk Yeomanry marched to Downham and then to Southery to quell the riots, but word had spread and the rioters had dispersed. However, many were arrested and some sent to Norwich Castle and others to Swaffham Bridewell where, presumably, they joined the poachers they were originally intent on freeing.

SWAFFHAM. *Norfolk.*
The Bridewell.

Keeper, *David Raven.*
  Salary, 70*l.* and one-fourth part of the Prisoners' earnings. No Fees.

Chaplain, Rev. Mr. *Chapman;* now Rev. *Wm. Johnson Jonge.* Salary, 30*l.*
  Duty, Prayers three times a week, and Sermon on Sundays.

Surgeon, Mr. *Law;* now Mr. *Ross;* who makes a Bill.

Number of Prisoners,
  1805, Sept. 2d, Seventeen. 1810, Sept. 5th, Seventeen.

Allowance, on Sunday, two pounds and two ounces of bread, with ox-cheek and soup for dinner.
  Monday, two pounds two ounces of bread.
  Tuesday, one pound and one ounce of bread, with a quart of pease-soup.
  Wednesday, Thursday, Friday, and *Saturday,* the same as on Tuesday.

REMARKS.

The Keeper's house fronts the Street, having behind it a court-yard 60 feet square, with a well in the centre, and two sewers and other conveniences on one side. The Keeper's rooms have a full view of the Prison in every part.

On the ground-floor of one side is a lobby, 42 feet long and 4 feet wide, into which open five cells; and at the end of the lobby is a small neat Chapel, of 18 feet by 12. The upper-story also has five cells; and at the end of the lobby is a work-room, of the same size as the Chapel.

The opposite side of the building has the like number of cells, opening into lobbies of the same dimensions with those before described; and also two end rooms set apart for Infirmaries. Each of the cells is 12 feet long by 7, with arched roof, and 9 feet 6 inches high; fitted up with crib bedsteads, straw-in-sacking, two sheets, two blankets, and a rug. They have spinning-wheels in them, and hemp-blocks; and are lighted and ventilated by an iron grated window, 28 inches square, with inside shutter, and a small aperture in each door, for the convenience of the Keeper.

The Rules and Orders are printed and hung up; but neither the Act for Preserving Health, nor the Clauses against Spirituous Liquors.

Those committed to hard labour have no part of their earnings. Those for Assaults, Bastardy, and Poaching, have one half. The average of annual Earnings is about *forty pounds.*

Employment, beating and dressing hemp, and spinning. The Prison very clean, and whitewashed once a year.

The condition of the prison they went to is described by this extract from the Report On Prisons published in 1810.

THE CAMPINGLAND

Leaving the Shirehall and its 150 year history of service to the community, and heading back towards the church, the open area of grassland known as the Campingland is on the right. Given to the town by the Rev Dr Botewright in 1463 for archery, running and military drill, by 1475 it was also being used for the rather boisterous game of Camp, a sort of early football. This was a game with three versions, the most violent of which was *'kicking camp'*, a no-holds barred game with the players not so much kicking the ball, as the name might suggest, but rather each other! This was allowed, as was punching and wrestling. Needless to say, this was frowned on by the church and most authorities, although the military encouraged it. As this land was the playground for two schools of boisterous boys between 1736 and 1955, it can be said that a version of football was played here in one form or another for 475 years. This must make the Campingland one of the oldest football pitches in existence!

On the Campingland is the Youth and Community Centre. This stands on the site of Hamond's Free School, which moved to the Market Place in 1901, occupying the old Norwich and Swaffham Bank premises. The school became a grammar school, and is now Swaffham Sixth Form Centre.

The Free School was founded in 1736 with £1,000 left in the will of Nicholas Hamond, Lord of the Manor of Swaffham, who lived in the Manor House. The school was *'to teach 20 poor boys reading'*. The Sixth Form Centre now has 125 students from as far afield as Watton. Hamond's High School in Brandon Road has about 600 pupils from the town and nearby villages. A far cry from the school envisaged by the philanthropic Nicholas Hamond 250 years ago!

NATIONAL SCHOOLS

Opposite the Youth and Community Centre is what is now the Parish Church Rooms, but if we look up it can be seen that this was the *'National School 1838'*. It was designed by the Swaffham born architect W J Donthorn. Boys were taught on the ground floor and girls on the first floor until 1901, when the girls had their own school in a new building on White Cross Road, next to the Infants' School.

Much could be written about the antics of the pupils here, but there is not enough room in this slender volume to recount all the adventures and misfortunes of Swaffham schoolchildren in Victorian times. However, a few details might prove of interest.

In the early days, the children came to the National School from the lower school housed in the old parish workhouse in the churchyard. This was run by Miss Hamond (again, of the Manor House) who seemed to be rather fond of her charges, because on one or two occasions Mr Pheasant, headmaster of the National School boys, commented that children were being kept at the lower school *'until they were nearly at an age when they would leave school to start work.'* The age referred to would be about nine years.

School in those days was very much religion-orientated. The boys of the National School would attend the parish church on every Saint's day and Sundays too of course. In fact, if a boy did not attend Sunday School, he was liable to be expelled from the weekday school. Nonconformists too had to attend the *'regular'* church or face expulsion from the school. As might be expected, the local clergy had a great say in the running of the school, and visited it at least once a week.

Finance for the school came from grants and school fees, which were one penny per week for the first child in a family, and half a penny for younger ones. The school managers decided that children from the workhouse would have to pay twice as much as other children. A curious state of affairs, considering the reason that many of these children were in the workhouse in the first place was because their parents were destitute. The school fees continued after the 1870 Education Act which made attendance compulsory.

Despite this Act, truancy was a common problem, especially when those fairs were in town. Also, at certain times of the year, it could be expected that some children would be away because of seasonal work such as osier peeling, walnut gathering and, of course, harvest time. To avoid too much absenteeism at harvest time, the school governors would adjust the summer holidays to fit in with the local harvest.

Bad weather too was a cause of absenteeism. Heavy rain, snow and ice caused children to stay away. This may seem surprising today, but when we consider that the roads were just dirt tracks and there was no school transport, so many children had to walk miles to school and in bad weather it was not uncommon for the town pit to flood right across the road, such absenteeism is understandable.

Snow and ice obviously posed yet more problems. There were not the vehicles then to clear the stuff away, just a man and a team of horses. Contemporary reports tell that some of the children suffered during this weather, because of the poverty and cold at home. More than once a child did not come to school because he could not get his boots on due to chilblains. One young man could not attend because his boots were at the menders and he had no others.

Clearing the snow on the Market Place by the Bagge Memorial.

The sort of conditions some of these children had to endure gave rise to other problems. Epidemics frequently swept through the town. Scarlet fever, cholera, measles and the lesser afflictions still with us, such as mumps, all appeared and the more serious ones frequently took their toll of young lives. On one or two occasions all the schools were closed for weeks because of measles epidemics. It was not uncommon for individual schools to close down for a while because of scarlet fever.

Insanitary conditions were a great cause of these epidemics. Frequently families drew their water from common public wells, although one doctor did ascribe the cause of a particularly widespread epidemic to *'drinking water from the taps'*. Whether he meant taps as we know them today or hand pumps outside, we cannot be sure, but as communal pumps were a source of disease, so poor drainage caused more trouble. In 1888 the Local Board (the predecessor of the Council) declared that the *'sewage ditch which ran past the Manor House and Keeper's Cottage, is foul and injurious to health'*. This ditch almost certainly drained into an open pond at the crossroads of Sporle Road and New Sporle Road. In wet weather this would regularly overflow across the road. Piped drains replaced the ditch the next year and in 1896 the new Urban District Council installed a complete new drainage system in the town at a cost of £2,300.

Overcrowding at home was another prime cause of infection spreading. For example, large families with aged parents as well as children often lived in small cottages with as few as two bedrooms reached by a ladder from one of the two downstairs rooms. These cottages were frequently crammed together in a small yard, with one outside toilet for two or three cottages. It was often reported that a particular yard had the fever and consequently all children there had to stay at home, because once it started, it only needed one infected child in the close-packed conditions at school for another epidemic to sweep the town.

BACK TO THE TOWN CENTRE

Next to the Church Rooms is the curiously-named Pightle. This name has its origins in the old English *'pight'*, which means to throw, especially a long pointed weapon, such as a pike. Therefore a *'pightle'* has come to mean a piece of ground longer than it is wide. In the 1845 map of Swaffham, there are many pightles listed, most being strips of agricultural land. This one in town is the only one remaining.

Just over half way down the Pightle is a date stone set in an old wall. This reads RG 1775. The RG was Robert Goodrick, who owned all the land on that side, up to the Campingland. At that end was a cavernous hole in the ground which used to be Mr Goodrick's brick-making works. Most of it is now filled in and built on. Mr Goodrick lived in Westgate House at the town end of the Pightle, and here John Wesley, the founder of the Methodist religion, preached from a window during one of his two visits to the town.

On the right, opposite Westgate House, is one end of a very old terrace dating back to the 17th century or earlier. Some of the many changes to this particular property can be seen in this end wall. A brick window or door arch now surrounds flints and mortar. More brickwork, possibly from an early gable, can be seen partially hidden in the ivy.

If we walk along to the other end of this terrace, a different wall is seen. This time all in brick, the outline of the original wall can clearly be made out. A much smaller building then, it was originally thatched. This we can tell by the comparatively high chimney outlined in the wall. The height was to enable the wind to carry the sparks from the chimney away from the thatch which could, and often did, catch light very easily.

Across the road is a reminder of this problem with thatch. High on the wall of the Co-Op is a carved stone head. Looking very much out of place on a modern building, it is a very significant stone, for this reputedly marks the point where the *'Great Fire of Swaffham'* was brought under control. *'The Great Fire'* started in the Blue Boar Inn and, fanned by a strong north wind, destroyed 22 properties and badly damaged two more before it was brought under control by the town's fire fighting equipment. This comprised two hand-pumped engines, 27 water buckets and two cromes (all kept in or by the church). All those plus, no doubt, various other buckets, pots, pans and anything that would hold water, were brought into action by almost 200 men.

The men formed a bucket chain across to the Town Pit and they must have been hard at work for hours trying to control the fire which was not only burning the thatch, but also the wooden frames of these old buildings. As was the custom at these times, beer and bread were available for the firefighters afterwards.

The contents of the destroyed properties were valued at over £800. Some people had a remarkable memory for the items they had lost, others either could not remember or did not have much in the first place. The latter is especially true of the servants who lost their possessions in this terrible blaze.

If the stone head does mark the end of the fire, then the properties involved must have been very small indeed for there to have been 22 on such a short length of road. That is, unless some of the businesses were in courtyards or at the back of others. As there are no plans of the area before the fire, we can only guess. After the fire, a by-law was passed prohibiting thatch from being used to roof the new properties.

Next to the Co-Op is the Town Hall, home of Swaffham Museum and the Town Council. It has not always been a civic building though. After the Great Fire it was the residence of John Morse, a brewer. The brewery stood behind the house and along Cley Road. It had grown to quite a substantial business by 1847, with 42 public houses belonging to the brewery, as far afield as Dereham, Thetford and King's Lynn. It continued in business until early this century, when the then owners, Steward & Patterson, closed their Swaffham branch.

Swaffham Town Hall – home of the Town Council and Swaffham Museum (Poppyland Photos)

Stone bottles labelled *'Steward & Patterson, Norwich & Swaffham, Ginger beer, 1d'*, can sometimes still be found in old rubbish tips.

Next to the Town Hall is the White Hart Inn. This was the Blue Boar Inn where the fire started. After the fire, the name was changed to the Black Horse, and then to the White Hart. In the 1960s the name was changed again, this time to The Breckland, but now it has reverted to the White Hart.

If we look around the Market Place, a few 20th century buildings can be seen, but the overall impression is that very little has changed during the past 200 years or more. True, the shop windows and doorways are modern, but above these most buildings remain much the same.

If we look around, trying to ignore the traffic, and imagining the whole Market Place as peaceful as the scene in these photographs of the Market Cross and Bagge Memorial, then we can understand the feelings that prompted the Rev Keeling-Scott, vicar of Swaffham 1908–1928, to write this poem.

The Market Cross – built by the Earl of Orford 1783

The Little Town Swaffham

Come with me
And see our little town.
'Tis very old and wide and brown.
A reddish brown below,
But up above, with tiles I love,
A burnt-up deeper brown.

The streets are wide
And still, and very empty,
People cross as if they crossed a room they know,
Filled with familiar furniture,
Without surprise or interest in their eyes,
As if at home.

Poem by Frederick Keeling-Scott, vicar of Swaffham 1908-1928 (left)

There's water in our market,
Shallow, still and brown;
And horses stop and stoop to drink,
And driver stops to light his pipe
And stare awhile and think;
There's leisure in our town.

Our shops are small
And rather frightened-looking;
Shyly they stand in ones and twos
Like girls along the wall,
Waiting for partners, who seldom come,
And when they come, refuse.

When evening comes,
The street-lamps twinkle, few
And very far apart
Lights shine from windows,
Eyes look out as if they knew
There's nothing much to see.

Night falls at last;
Our town has gone to rest.
Beside the Market Cross
A policeman stands on guard,
Watching the shadows. Within the stable-yard,
A lone cat yawns. The clock strikes ten –
Our town's asleep.

The Bagge Memorial – built by public subscription in 1882 in honour of Sir William Bagge MP. Demolished in 1940 after severe winter damage. (below)

NOTABLE SWAFFHAM PEOPLE

If we walk down Mangate Street, past the church on the right and the Convent of the Sacred Heart on the left, past the Town Pound and the row of cottages dating from 1730, and the Manor Farm, and turn left past the Manor House, a small cottage is arrived at beside a public footpath. This cottage is Keeper's Cottage, and was the birthplace of Samuel John Carter, a notable Victorian animal artist.

Samuel John's talent was apparent from an early age, as can be seen from his drawing of the Old Vicarage made when he was only 11 years old. It was this sort of work that prompted his father's employers, the Hamond family of the Manor House, to pay for the boy to attend the Royal Academy School in London, where he won a silver medal during his first term.

The young Howard Carter, aged 8, drawn by William Carter (Courtesy of Mr J Carter)

Samuel John Carter (Courtesy Mr A Carter)

On leaving the Academy, Samuel became a professional artist, working both in London and in Norfolk, painting the animals of the gentry. While in London, it is said that Carter worked for Landseer for a time, and it is family tradition that Samuel made the original drawings for the lions at the base of Nelson's Column in Trafalgar Square.

Samuel married a Swaffham girl, Martha Joyce Sands, the daughter of a builder in Lynn Street. He was quite a successful artist and built a house for his family near Sporle Road. As Samuel and his family were in London a lot of the time, his two sisters lived in the Swaffham house.

It was to this house and the care of his two aunts, that the youngest of Samuel's 11 children, Howard, was brought when he was just an infant. A sickly child, the young Carter was raised without the rough and tumble other boys enjoyed on the sportsfield or on the local playgrounds.

We do not know anything of Howard Carter's education, but it is believed to have been private. What we do know is that when his father was working from his Swaffham house, young Howard would go with him and learn the skills of the professional artist as he watched his father paint for the local gentry.

Didlington Hall – country home of William Amhurst Tyssen Amhurst, who inspired Howard Carter's interest in Egypt. (above)

Howard Carter in Swaffham on holiday from Egypt, 1901 (right)

One of these country houses visited by the Carters was Didlington Hall, seat of William Amhurst Tyssen Amhurst MP, later Lord Amherst of Hackney. Here young Howard was allowed to visit the many rooms that had been converted into museums. One of the most influential in Howard's life was the Egyptian Room, for Mr Amhurst was a keen collector of Egyptian artefacts and these fascinated Howard.

In 1890 the Amhursts had a visit from Percy Newberry, an Egyptologist who worked for the Egypt Exploration Fund, of which Mr Amhurst was a committee member. Mr Newberry needed help with some drawings at the British Museum and Mrs Amhurst suggested the 17 year old Howard Carter, a very good artist, who was interested in history and in Egypt. Newberry liked Carter's work and gave him a job for three months in the British Museum. Those three months turned into several years, for the next year the talented young Carter was out in Egypt, copying tomb and other wall paintings. He quickly gained a reputation as the premier epigraphist of his day and worked on important sites with the greatest Egyptologists of the 19th century. Thus started a brilliant career in archaeology which reached its peak in 1922 when Howard Carter discovered the tomb of the boy-king Tutankhamun. The story of the discovery and the subsequent ten years of careful excavation is so well known and has taken up so many specialist books, that if more details are required, it is suggested that a search in the local library would be helpful. Suffice to say that the man who found the world's greatest archaeological treasure against all odds, was a Swaffham man and the town in rightly proud of him.

Howard was not the only one of Samuel's children to do well. Sister Amy was an accomplished miniaturist and brother Verney was an engraver who designed a World War I medal. Another brother, William, went to the Royal Academy School as his father had before him, and went on to become a very accomplished portrait painter. Portraits by William of the Earl of Caernarvon and Howard Carter hang in Highclere Castle.

Leaving the Keeper's Cottage, the road soon reaches a crossroads. The road to the right leads past Sporle Road House, while the road to the left sweeps up a gentle hill back to the town. This is the road to take.

On the way, the Drill Hall is soon seen on the right. In this building is housed the regimental museum of the Suffolk and Norfolk Yeomanry and the weapons of the Territorial Army, the modern-day successors to the Yeomanry.

Further along is Swaffham Cottage Hospital, founded in 1887 to commemorate the Golden Jubilee of Queen Victoria. Generously supported by the town, the patients here are well provided for by the community. The Swaffham Hospital Cup is said to be the oldest amateur charity football competition still run under the auspices of the Football Association.

The Cottage Hospital around the turn of the century.

Sir Arthur Knyvet Wilson Bt, VC, GCB, OM, GCVO, DCL.

At the top of the road, again on the right hand side, is Beech House. This was the home of Admiral of the Fleet, the late Sir Arthur Knyvet Wilson Bt, VC, GCB, OM, GCVO, DCL, whose grandfather was vicar of Swaffham for 65 years. Sir Arthur was born in the town on 4th March 1842 and won his Victoria Cross on the 29th February 1884 at El Teb (see citation) while he was captain of HMS Hecla. Captain Knyvet Wilson was presented with a sword by the officers of the torpedo school to mark his achievement. He is one of a very few Royal Navy officers to win the Victoria Cross.

On his return to his home town after this heroic battle, he was greeted at the railway station by a vast crowd. The gentry in their carriages, pensioners wearing their medals, the local volunteers with a band, ordinary folk and the children, who had been given a half-day holiday from school for this occasion, all formed a procession which carried him along to his mother's house. The railway station and town were decorated with flags and banners and the shops were closed for the occasion.

A strict disciplinarian, Sir Arthur was known as *'Old 'ard 'eart'* to his sailors, who nevertheless held him in great respect. He was responsible for several inventions and innovations during a time when steam-driven ironclads were taking over from wooden hulled sailing ships. Inventions such as the truck semaphore, submarine mines, sea heliograph, a device to enable torpedoes to cut through protective netting around ships and an instrument to improve gun aiming are amongst them.

Sir Arthur's memorial and citation.

Improvements made by Wilson were many and included modifications which enabled torpedoes to be launched underwater from a ship moving at high speed. This was described as *'the most important advance made during the year'* (1888).

Sir Arthur first served on the *'Victory'*, rose through the ranks and was an admiral when he was due to retire in 1907. However, a special Order in Council gave him five more years of service. He afterwards spent two years in retirement in Swaffham, and was then offered the post of First Sea Lord in succession to Lord Fisher. It seems he was reluctant to accept this post, and only did so after strong pressure from King Edward VII.

He retired once more to Swaffham, but in 1915 Winston Churchill called him out of retirement to help to lead the Navy through the Great War. Retiring yet again in 1918, Sir Arthur became involved in local works. He helped to design the golf course, the stained glass memorial window and tablet in the Corpus Christi Chapel in the parish church, and Swaffham War Memorial, frequently using his own money to help finance the projects.

Sir Arthur Knyvet Wilson died on Wednesday 21st May 1921 and is buried in Swaffham churchyard. A memorial plaque and copy of the great man's Victoria Cross citation are in the church. With such a splendid service career, *'Tug'* Wilson ranks alongside that other Norfolk sailor, Nelson.

Turning left again, the road leads back to the town centre through what was the fashionable part of the town during the 18th century. The elegant houses clustered around here bear witness to this.

Very soon the church comes into view again, obscured partly by the many fine trees in the churchyard. Earlier this century when this photograph was taken the view was much more open. We can also see on the photo a small square construction on the traffic island in front of the George Hotel. This small

One of the public wells in front of the parish church.

building covered a public well, which was maintained at the expense of the parish. There were a few public wells around the Market Place; others stood down Lynn Street, near the Greyhound Inn and in the Shambles.

Also in the same picture on the road can be seen the reason for a local occupation which brought revenue to the town rather than expense. A 'scavenger' cleaned the streets behind the horses and other animals and his collected material was piled up in the Shambles until enough was accumulated to sell to local farmers. The word 'shambles' originally meant a butchery, or covered meat market. Whether there were still butcher's shops there when the scavenger was using the Shambles, we are not sure. For the right to scavenge the streets, a fee had to be paid to the council.

Across the road from The George Hotel, steps lead once more into the churchyard. It was in this corner that the old vicarage stood until 1847. It had its own well which is said to still exist, although now cleverly disguised as a tomb!

The fate of this vicarage was decided by Rev Sailsbury Everard who, upon becoming vicar in 1845, decided that the premises did not meet his requirements. He built a grand new vicarage on glebe land adjoining the Campingland. The town was obliged to purchase the old property from the vicar and demolish it, in order to create more space for burials in the crowded churchyard. The cost of this was over £700, but the money was raised by selling off some of the common land to the new railways. Thus the town gained half an acre or less of burial ground for the loss of nineteen acres of common land.

And so we arrive back at the church, where our journey began. There is much more history to Swaffham than I have been able to touch on here, but I hope this little introduction to our town has been of interest. If so, Swaffham Museum has many items of local history to help you appreciate and learn about the town that is Swaffham – the most beautiful market town in Norfolk.

1797 Map of Swaffham by Faden

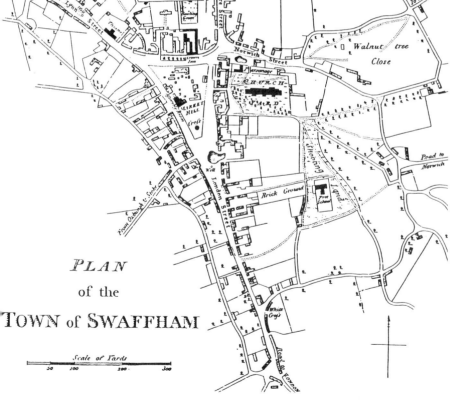

BIBLIOGRAPHY

Ribbons From the Pedlar's Pack, Ben Ripper (1972)

Pride of Swaffham, W B Rix (1950)

Bygone Gleanings and Present, W B Rix (1931)

History of Norfolk, Vol VI, F Blomefield (1807)

Life of Admiral Sir Arthur Knyvet Wilson, Admiral Sir Edward Bradford (1923)

An Account of the Swaffham Guilds, W H K (1833)

An Account of Swaffham Markets and Fairs, W H K (1833)

(The date of 1833 given to the two publications by W H K above are approximate dates given by W B Rix. W H K is believed to be W H Kemble, a Swaffham printer and bookseller).

Minute book of the Swaffham Local Board May 1880 – April 1890 at Norfolk Records Office Ref No DC14/1/3

Swaffham Wesleyan Methodist Chapel in 1898. During this century three lay preachers from this chapel have become members of Parliament: William Taylor JP, Sidney Dye JP, and Albert (later Lord) Hilton